The *Address* & *Telephone* *Book*

Full-page photographs
National Trust Photographic Library, © National Trust 1992:
Neil Campbell-Sharp pages 8, 10, 14, 16, 44, 70, 80, 86, 88, 92,
104, 116, 134, 136, 140, 142; Jerry Harpur pages 46, 98, 110; Ian
Shaw page 50; George Wright page 128. *The Garden Picture
Library*: Brigitte Thomas pages 38, 62, 76; John Glover page 26;
Ron Sutherland page 40; Gary Rogers page 56. *Harry Smith
Collection*: pages 32, 82, 122, 130. *Heather Angel*: pages 4, 68,
112. *Ardea London Ltd*: François Gohier page 100. *David Squire*:
page 22. Remainder of full-page photographs: Neil Sutherland.

Cut-out photographs
Neil Sutherland

Jacket photography
Neil Sutherland

Design
Paul Turner and Sue Pressley, Stonecastle Graphics Ltd;
Nigel Duffield

Managing Editor
Jo Finnis

Production
Ruth Arthur
Sally Connolly
Andrew Whitelaw
Neil Randles

Production Director
Gerald Hughes

Cover: National Trust Photographic Library/
Neil Cambell-Sharp
16247 The Address & Telephone Book
This edition published in 1997 by Bramley
Distributed in the USA by BHB International Inc.,
30 Edison Drive, Wayne, New Jersey 07470
© 1992 Waverley 1770
All rights reserved
Printed and bound in Singapore

ISBN 1-85833-686-4

The *Address* & *Telephone* *Book*

Bramley

Water lily (*Nymphaea 'Attraction'*)

Name

Telephone

Address

Fax

Name

Telephone

Address

Fax

Name

Telephone

Address

Fax

Name

Telephone

Address

Fax

Name

Telephone

Address

Fax

A

Name	*Telephone*
Address	
	Fax

Name	*Telephone*
Address	
	Fax

Name	*Telephone*
Address	
	Fax

Name	*Telephone*
Address	
	Fax

Name	*Telephone*
Address	
	Fax

Name

Address

Telephone

Fax

Name

Address

Telephone

Fax

Name

Address

Telephone

Fax

Name

Address

Telephone

Fax

Name

Address

Telephone

Fax

A

Apple and cherry trees in full blossom

Name

Address

Telephone

Fax

Name

Address

Telephone

Fax

Name

Address

Telephone

Fax

Name

Address

Telephone

Fax

Name

Address

Telephone

Fax

Spiderwort or trinity flower (*Tradescantia x andersoniana*)

Name

Telephone

Address

Fax

Name

Telephone

Address

Fax

Name

Telephone

Address

Fax

Name

Telephone

Address

Fax

Name

Telephone

Address

Fax

B

Name	Telephone
Address	
	Fax

Name	Telephone
Address	
	Fax

Name	Telephone
Address	
	Fax

Name	Telephone
Address	
	Fax

Name	Telephone
Address	
	Fax

Name	Telephone
Address	
	Fax

Name	Telephone
Address	
	Fax

Name	Telephone
Address	
	Fax

Name	Telephone
Address	
	Fax

Name	Telephone
Address	
	Fax

B

French lavender *(Lavandula stoechas)*

Name

Telephone

Address

Fax

Name

Telephone

Address

Fax

Name

Telephone

Address

Fax

Name

Telephone

Address

Fax

Name

Telephone

Address

Fax

Peony *(Paeonia lactiflora)*

Name

Telephone

Address

Fax

Name

Telephone

Address

Fax

Name

Telephone

Address

Fax

Name

Telephone

Address

Fax

Name

Telephone

Address

Fax

C

Name ....

Address ....

....

....

Telephone ....

....

Fax ....

....

Name ....

Address ....

....

....

Telephone ....

....

Fax ....

....

Name ....

Address ....

....

....

Telephone ....

....

Fax ....

....

Name ....

Address ....

....

....

Telephone ....

....

Fax ....

....

Name ....

Address ....

....

....

Telephone ....

....

Fax ....

....

C

Name

Address

Telephone

Fax

Name

Address

Telephone

Fax

Name

Address

Telephone

Fax

Name

Address

Telephone

Fax

Name

Address

Telephone

Fax

C

Damask violet or sweet rocket (*Hesperis matronalis*)

Name	Telephone
Address	
	Fax

Name	Telephone
Address	
	Fax

Name	Telephone
Address	
	Fax

Name	Telephone
Address	
	Fax

Name	Telephone
Address	
	Fax

Rose (*Rosa canina* 'Abbotswood')

D

Name	Telephone
Address	
	Fax

Name	Telephone
Address	
	Fax

Name	Telephone
Address	
	Fax

Name	Telephone
Address	
	Fax

Name	Telephone
Address	
	Fax

D

Name	*Telephone*
Address	
	Fax

Name	*Telephone*
Address	
	Fax

Name	*Telephone*
Address	
	Fax

Name	*Telephone*
Address	
	Fax

Name	*Telephone*
Address	
	Fax

Name

Telephone

Address

Fax

Name

Telephone

Address

Fax

Name

Telephone

Address

Fax

Name

Telephone

Address

Fax

Name

Telephone

Address

Fax

D

Astilbe

Name	*Telephone*
Address	
	Fax

Name	*Telephone*
Address	
	Fax

Name	*Telephone*
Address	
	Fax

Name	*Telephone*
Address	
	Fax

Name	*Telephone*
Address	
	Fax

Poppy *(Papaver rhoeas)*

E

Name	Telephone
Address	
	Fax

Name	Telephone
Address	
	Fax

Name	Telephone
Address	
	Fax

Name	Telephone
Address	
	Fax

Name	Telephone
Address	
	Fax

E

Name

Telephone

Address

Fax

Name

Telephone

Address

Fax

Name

Telephone

Address

Fax

Name

Telephone

Address

Fax

Name

Telephone

Address

Fax

Name

Telephone

Address

Fax

Name

Telephone

Address

Fax

Name

Telephone

Address

Fax

Name

Telephone

Address

Fax

Name

Telephone

Address

Fax

Azalea *(Rhododendron)*

Name

Telephone

Address

Fax

Name

Telephone

Address

Fax

Name

Telephone

Address

Fax

Name

Telephone

Address

Fax

Name

Telephone

Address

Fax

F

Dahlia 'Dana Peach'

F

Name	*Telephone*
Address	
	Fax

Name	*Telephone*
Address	
	Fax

Name	*Telephone*
Address	
	Fax

Name	*Telephone*
Address	
	Fax

Name	*Telephone*
Address	
	Fax

F

Name	Telephone
Address	
	Fax

Name	Telephone
Address	
	Fax

Name	Telephone
Address	
	Fax

Name	Telephone
Address	
	Fax

Name	Telephone
Address	
	Fax

Name	Telephone
Address	
	Fax

Name	Telephone
Address	
	Fax

Name	Telephone
Address	
	Fax

Name	Telephone
Address	
	Fax

Name	Telephone
Address	
	Fax

F

Yellow rhododendron and primulas

Name	Telephone
Address	
	Fax

Name	Telephone
Address	
	Fax

Name	Telephone
Address	
	Fax

Name	Telephone
Address	
	Fax

Name	Telephone
Address	
	Fax

G

Foxglove *(Digitalis purpurea)*

Name	Telephone
Address	
	Fax

G

Name	Telephone
Address	
	Fax

Name	Telephone
Address	
	Fax

Name	Telephone
Address	
	Fax

Name	Telephone
Address	
	Fax

Name	*Telephone*
Address	
	Fax

Name	*Telephone*
Address	
	Fax

Name	*Telephone*
Address	
	Fax

Name	*Telephone*
Address	
	Fax

Name	*Telephone*
Address	
	Fax

Name	Telephone
Address	
	Fax

Name	Telephone
Address	
	Fax

Name	Telephone
Address	
	Fax

Name	Telephone
Address	
	Fax

Name	Telephone
Address	
	Fax

Eryngium

Name
....

Address
....

....

....

Telephone
....

....

Fax
....

....

Name
....

Address
....

....

....

Telephone
....

....

Fax
....

....

Name
....

Address
....

....

....

Telephone
....

....

Fax
....

....

Name
....

Address
....

....

....

Telephone
....

....

Fax
....

....

Name
....

Address
....

....

....

Telephone
....

....

Fax
....

....

H

Blue poppy (*Meconopsis betonicifolia*)

Name	Telephone
Address	
	Fax

Name	Telephone
Address	
	Fax

H

Name	Telephone
Address	
	Fax

Name	Telephone
Address	
	Fax

Name	Telephone
Address	
	Fax

Name	Telephone
Address	
	Fax

Name	Telephone
Address	
	Fax

Name	Telephone
Address	
	Fax

Name	Telephone
Address	
	Fax

Name	Telephone
Address	
	Fax

Name	Telephone
Address	
	Fax

Name	Telephone
Address	
	Fax

Name	Telephone
Address	
	Fax

Name	Telephone
Address	
	Fax

Name	Telephone
Address	
	Fax

Carpet of bluebells or wild hyacinths *(Endymion nonscriptus)*

Name

Telephone

Address

Fax

Name

Telephone

Address

Fax

Name

Telephone

Address

Fax

Name

Telephone

Address

Fax

Name

Telephone

Address

Fax

Mallow *(Lavatera trimestris)*

Name	*Telephone*
Address	
	Fax

Name	*Telephone*
Address	
	Fax

I

Name	*Telephone*
Address	
	Fax

Name	*Telephone*
Address	
	Fax

Name	*Telephone*
Address	
	Fax

I

Name	*Telephone*
Address	
	Fax

Name	*Telephone*
Address	
	Fax

Name	*Telephone*
Address	
	Fax

Name	*Telephone*
Address	
	Fax

Name	*Telephone*
Address	
	Fax

Name

Telephone

Address

Fax

Name

Telephone

Address

Fax

Name

Telephone

Address

Fax

Name

Telephone

Address

Fax

Name

Telephone

Address

Fax

Hydrangea macrophylla

Name
....

Telephone
....

Address
....

....

Fax
....

....

....

....

Name
....

Telephone
....

Address
....

....

Fax
....

....

....

....

Name
....

Telephone
....

Address
....

....

Fax
....

....

....

....

Name
....

Telephone
....

Address
....

....

Fax
....

....

....

....

Name
....

Telephone
....

Address
....

....

Fax
....

....

....

....

Tulip (*Tulipa*)

Name	*Telephone*
Address	
	Fax

Name	*Telephone*
Address	
	Fax

J

Name	*Telephone*
Address	
	Fax

Name	*Telephone*
Address	
	Fax

Name	*Telephone*
Address	
	Fax

J

Name .... Telephone ....

Address ....

.... Fax ....

....

....

Name .... Telephone ....

Address ....

.... Fax ....

....

....

Name .... Telephone ....

Address ....

.... Fax ....

....

....

Name .... Telephone ....

Address ....

.... Fax ....

....

....

Name .... Telephone ....

Address ....

.... Fax ....

....

....

Name .... Telephone ....

Address ....

.... Fax ....

....

....

Name .... Telephone ....

Address ....

.... Fax ....

....

....

Name .... Telephone ....

Address ....

.... Fax ....

....

....

Name .... Telephone ....

Address ....

.... Fax ....

....

....

Name .... Telephone ....

Address ....

.... Fax ....

....

Poppies *(Papaver rhoeas)*

Name

Telephone

Address

Fax

Name

Telephone

Address

Fax

Name

Telephone

Address

Fax

Name

Telephone

Address

Fax

Name

Telephone

Address

Fax

K

Dahlia

Name	Telephone
Address	
	Fax

Name	Telephone
Address	
	Fax

K

Name	Telephone
Address	
	Fax

Name	Telephone
Address	
	Fax

Name	Telephone
Address	
	Fax

K

Name	*Telephone*
Address	
	Fax

Name	*Telephone*
Address	
	Fax

Name	*Telephone*
Address	
	Fax

Name	*Telephone*
Address	
	Fax

Name	*Telephone*
Address	
	Fax

Name

Telephone

Address

Fax

Name

Telephone

Address

Fax

Name

Telephone

Address

Fax

Name

Telephone

Address

Fax

Name

Telephone

Address

Fax

Acer japonicum 'Vitifolium'

Name

Telephone

Address

Fax

Name

Telephone

Address

Fax

Name

Telephone

Address

Fax

Name

Telephone

Address

Fax

Name

Telephone

Address

Fax

L

Bird of paradise flower (*Strelitzia reginae*)

Name	Telephone
Address	
	Fax

Name	Telephone
Address	
	Fax

Name	Telephone
Address	
	Fax

L

Name	Telephone
Address	
	Fax

Name	Telephone
Address	
	Fax

L

Name	Telephone
Address	
	Fax

Name	Telephone
Address	
	Fax

Name	Telephone
Address	
	Fax

Name	Telephone
Address	
	Fax

Name	Telephone
Address	
	Fax

Name	Telephone
Address	
	Fax

Name	Telephone
Address	
	Fax

Name	Telephone
Address	
	Fax

Name	Telephone
Address	
	Fax

Name	Telephone
Address	
	Fax

Helenium autumnale

Name ....

Telephone ....

Address ....

....

Fax ....

....

....

....

Name ....

Telephone ....

Address ....

....

Fax ....

....

....

....

Name ....

Telephone ....

Address ....

....

Fax ....

....

....

....

Name ....

Telephone ....

Address ....

....

Fax ....

....

....

....

Name ....

Telephone ....

Address ....

....

Fax ....

....

....

....

M

Potted pelargoniums and Virginia creeper *(Parthenocissus tricuspidata)*

Name	*Telephone*
Address	
	Fax

Name	*Telephone*
Address	
	Fax

Name	*Telephone*
Address	
	Fax

M

Name	*Telephone*
Address	
	Fax

Name	*Telephone*
Address	
	Fax

Name	*Telephone*
Address	
	Fax

Name	*Telephone*
Address	
	Fax

Name	*Telephone*
Address	
	Fax

Name	*Telephone*
Address	
	Fax

Name	*Telephone*
Address	
	Fax

Name

Telephone

Address

Fax

Name

Telephone

Address

Fax

Name

Telephone

Address

Fax

Name

Telephone

Address

Fax

Name

Telephone

Address

Fax

Teasel (*Dipsacus fullonum*)

Name

Telephone

Address

Fax

Name

Telephone

Address

Fax

Name

Telephone

Address

Fax

Name

Telephone

Address

Fax

Name

Telephone

Address

Fax

N

Orchid (*Vanda Thonglor*)

Name	Telephone
Address	
	Fax

Name	Telephone
Address	
	Fax

Name	Telephone
Address	
	Fax

Name	Telephone
Address	
	Fax

Name	Telephone
Address	
	Fax

N

N

Name

Telephone

Address

Fax

Name

Telephone

Address

Fax

Name

Telephone

Address

Fax

Name

Telephone

Address

Fax

Name

Telephone

Address

Fax

Name

Telephone

Address

Fax

Name

Telephone

Address

Fax

Name

Telephone

Address

Fax

Name

Telephone

Address

Fax

Name

Telephone

Address

Fax

Iris

Name	Telephone
Address	
	Fax

Name	Telephone
Address	
	Fax

Name	Telephone
Address	
	Fax

Name	Telephone
Address	
	Fax

Name	Telephone
Address	
	Fax

Camellia

Name	Telephone
Address	
	Fax

Name	Telephone
Address	
	Fax

Name	Telephone
Address	
	Fax

Name	Telephone
Address	
	Fax

Name	Telephone
Address	
	Fax

O

Name
....

Address
....

....

....

Telephone
....

Fax
....

....

Name
....

Address
....

....

....

Telephone
....

Fax
....

....

Name
....

Address
....

....

....

Telephone
....

Fax
....

....

Name
....

Address
....

....

....

Telephone
....

Fax
....

....

Name
....

Address
....

....

....

Telephone
....

Fax
....

....

O

Name	Telephone
Address	
	Fax

Name	Telephone
Address	
	Fax

Name	Telephone
Address	
	Fax

Name	Telephone
Address	
	Fax

Name	Telephone
Address	
	Fax

Apple blossom

Name	*Telephone*
Address	
	Fax

Name	*Telephone*
Address	
	Fax

Name	*Telephone*
Address	
	Fax

Name	*Telephone*
Address	
	Fax

Name	*Telephone*
Address	
	Fax

Anemone

Name	Telephone
Address	
	Fax

Name	Telephone
Address	
	Fax

Name	Telephone
Address	
	Fax

Name	Telephone
Address	
	Fax

P

Name	Telephone
Address	
	Fax

P

Name

Address

Telephone

Fax

Name

Address

Telephone

Fax

Name

Address

Telephone

Fax

Name

Address

Telephone

Fax

Name

Address

Telephone

Fax

Name		Telephone
Address		
		Fax

Name		Telephone
Address		
		Fax

Name		Telephone
Address		
		Fax

Name		Telephone
Address		
		Fax

Name		Telephone
Address		
		Fax

P

Embothrium coccineuiti

Name

Telephone

Address

Fax

Name

Telephone

Address

Fax

Name

Telephone

Address

Fax

Name

Telephone

Address

Fax

Name

Telephone

Address

Fax

Californian poppy *(Eschscholzia californica)*

Name	Telephone
Address	
	Fax

Name	Telephone
Address	
	Fax

Name	Telephone
Address	
	Fax

Name	Telephone
Address	
	Fax

Name	Telephone
Address	
	Fax

Q

Q

Name	*Telephone*
Address	
	Fax

Name	*Telephone*
Address	
	Fax

Name	*Telephone*
Address	
	Fax

Name	*Telephone*
Address	
	Fax

Name	*Telephone*
Address	
	Fax

Name	Telephone
Address	
	Fax

Name	Telephone
Address	
	Fax

Name	Telephone
Address	
	Fax

Name	Telephone
Address	
	Fax

Name	Telephone
Address	
	Fax

Fuchsia 'Mrs Popple'

Name	*Telephone*
Address	
	Fax

Name	*Telephone*
Address	
	Fax

Name	*Telephone*
Address	
	Fax

Name	*Telephone*
Address	
	Fax

Name	*Telephone*
Address	
	Fax

Sunflower *(Helianthus)*

Name	Telephone
Address	
	Fax

Name	Telephone
Address	
	Fax

Name	Telephone
Address	
	Fax

Name	Telephone
Address	
	Fax

R

Name	Telephone
Address	
	Fax

R

Name	Telephone
Address	
	Fax

Name	Telephone
Address	
	Fax

Name	Telephone
Address	
	Fax

Name	Telephone
Address	
	Fax

Name	Telephone
Address	
	Fax

Name

Telephone

Address

Fax

Name

Telephone

Address

Fax

Name

Telephone

Address

Fax

Name

Telephone

Address

Fax

Name

Telephone

Address

Fax

Azaleas *(Rhododendron)* and bluebells or wild hyacinths *(Endymion nonscriptus)*

Name	Telephone
Address	
	Fax

Name	Telephone
Address	
	Fax

Name	Telephone
Address	
	Fax

Name	Telephone
Address	
	Fax

Name	Telephone
Address	
	Fax

Iris 'Snowshill'

Name	Telephone
Address	
	Fax

Name	Telephone
Address	
	Fax

Name	Telephone
Address	
	Fax

Name	Telephone
Address	
	Fax

S

Name	Telephone
Address	
	Fax

S

Name

Telephone

Address

Fax

Name

Telephone

Address

Fax

Name

Telephone

Address

Fax

Name

Telephone

Address

Fax

Name

Telephone

Address

Fax

Name

Telephone

Address

Fax

Name

Telephone

Address

Fax

Name

Telephone

Address

Fax

Name

Telephone

Address

Fax

Name

Telephone

Address

Fax

Cosmea *(Cosmos bipinnatus)*

Name

Telephone

Address

Fax

Name

Telephone

Address

Fax

Name

Telephone

Address

Fax

Name

Telephone

Address

Fax

Name

Telephone

Address

Fax

Brunfelsia pauciflora calycina

Name	Telephone
Address	
	Fax

Name	Telephone
Address	
	Fax

Name	Telephone
Address	
	Fax

Name	Telephone
Address	
	Fax

Name	Telephone
Address	
	Fax

T

T

Name

Telephone

Address

Fax

Name

Telephone

Address

Fax

Name

Telephone

Address

Fax

Name

Telephone

Address

Fax

Name

Telephone

Address

Fax

Name	*Telephone*
Address	
	Fax

Name	*Telephone*
Address	
	Fax

Name	*Telephone*
Address	
	Fax

Name	*Telephone*
Address	
	Fax

Name	*Telephone*
Address	
	Fax

T

Canterbury bell *(Campanula medium)*

T

Name ....

Telephone ....

Address ....

Fax ....

....

....

Name ....

Telephone ....

Address ....

Fax ....

....

....

Name ....

Telephone ....

Address ....

Fax ....

....

....

Name ....

Telephone ....

Address ....

Fax ....

....

....

Name ....

Telephone ....

Address ....

Fax ....

....

....

U V

Kaffir lily *(Schizostylis coccinea)*

Name	Telephone
Address	
	Fax

Name	Telephone
Address	
	Fax

Name	Telephone
Address	
	Fax

Name	Telephone
Address	
	Fax

Name	Telephone
Address	
	Fax

UV

Name	*Telephone*
Address	
	Fax

Name	*Telephone*
Address	
	Fax

Name	*Telephone*
Address	
	Fax

Name	*Telephone*
Address	
	Fax

Name	*Telephone*
Address	
	Fax

Name	Telephone
Address	
	Fax

Name	Telephone
Address	
	Fax

Name	Telephone
Address	
	Fax

Name	Telephone
Address	
	Fax

Name	Telephone
Address	
	Fax

Pelargonium

Name

Telephone

Address

Fax

Name

Telephone

Address

Fax

Name

Telephone

Address

Fax

Name

Telephone

Address

Fax

Name

Telephone

Address

Fax

Field poppy *(Papaver rhoeas)*

Name	Telephone
Address	
	Fax

Name	Telephone
Address	
	Fax

Name	Telephone
Address	
	Fax

Name	Telephone
Address	
	Fax

Name	Telephone
Address	
	Fax

W

Name ....

Telephone ....

Address ....

....

Fax

....

....

....

....

Name ....

Telephone ....

Address ....

....

Fax

....

....

....

....

Name ....

Telephone ....

Address ....

....

Fax

....

....

....

....

Name ....

Telephone ....

Address ....

....

Fax

....

....

....

....

Name ....

Telephone ....

Address ....

....

Fax

....

....

Name	*Telephone*
Address	
	Fax

Name	*Telephone*
Address	
	Fax

Name	*Telephone*
Address	
	Fax

Name	*Telephone*
Address	
	Fax

Name	*Telephone*
Address	
	Fax

Spindle tree *(Euonymus alatus)*

Name

Address

Telephone

Fax

Name

Address

Telephone

Fax

Name

Address

Telephone

Fax

Name

Address

Telephone

Fax

Name

Address

Telephone

Fax

XY

Chinese lantern *(Physalis alkekengi)*

Name ....

Telephone ....

Address ....

....

Fax ....

....

Name ....

Telephone ....

Address ....

....

Fax ....

....

Name ....

Telephone ....

Address ....

....

Fax ....

....

Name ....

Telephone ....

Address ....

....

Fax ....

....

Name ....

Telephone ....

Address ....

....

Fax ....

....

XY

Name .... *Telephone* ....

Address ....

.... *Fax* ....

....

....

Name .... *Telephone* ....

Address ....

.... *Fax* ....

....

....

Name .... *Telephone* ....

Address ....

.... *Fax* ....

....

....

Name .... *Telephone* ....

Address ....

.... *Fax* ....

....

....

Name .... *Telephone* ....

Address ....

.... *Fax* ....

....

....

Name ....   Telephone ....

Address ....

....   Fax ....

....

....

Name ....   Telephone ....

Address ....

....   Fax ....

....

....

Name ....   Telephone ....

Address ....

....   Fax ....

....

....

Name ....   Telephone ....

Address ....

....   Fax ....

....

....

Name ....   Telephone ....

Address ....

....   Fax ....

....

Rowan or mountain ash *(Sorbus aucuparia)*

Name

Address

Telephone

Fax

Name

Address

Telephone

Fax

Name

Address

Telephone

Fax

Name

Address

Telephone

Fax

Name

Address

Telephone

Fax

Lantana vibernum